Word Problems from Literature

STUDENT WORKBOOK

A PLAYFUL MATH SINGLE

Word Problems from Literature

STUDENT WORKBOOK

Denise Gaskins

TABLETOP ACADEMY PRESS

Tabletop Academy Press, Blue Mound, IL, USA
tabletopacademy.net

ISBN: 978-1-892083-35-7

CREDITS:

"There are two ways …" Raoul Bott, quoted in The MacTutor History of
Mathematics archive.
www-history.mcs.st-and.ac.uk/Biographies/Bott.html

Mr. Popper's Penguins ©1938 Richard and Florence Atwater
Poor Richard ©1941 James Daugherty
The Lion, the Witch and the Wardrobe ©1949 C. S. Lewis
The Hobbit ©1937 J. R. R. Tolkien
The Lord of the Rings ©1954 J. R. R. Tolkien
Star Wars ©1977 George Lucas, 20th Century Fox
Dealing with Dragons ©1990 Patricia C. Wrede
Cover art copyright © SergeyNivens/DepositPhoto
Books and scroll art copyright © Macrovector/DepositPhoto
Penguin photo copyright © Javarman/DepositPhoto
Ben Franklin art copyright © Patrimonio/DepositPhoto
Lion photo copyright © Lifeonwhite/DepositPhoto
Dragon art copyright © Gurbi4/DepositPhoto
Orc Warrior art copyright © Denise Gaskins
Boys on Grid photo copyright © Denise Gaskins

There are two ways to do great mathematics.

The first is to be smarter than everybody else.

The second way is to be stupider than everybody else,
but persistent.

—RAOUL BOTT

Contents

Word Problems from Literature

Bar Model Diagrams as Pictorial Manipulatives

BAR MODEL DIAGRAMS ARE ALGEBRA in pictures. We show all the known and unknown parts of our story as block-like rectangles. Then we imagine moving the blocks around or cutting them into smaller pieces until we can figure out the unknown parts.

Bar models transform the abstract mystery of the word problem into a shape puzzle: how can we fit these blocks together? This helps us notice the underlying structure of a word problem, so we can see how this problem is like others we've already solved.

It's almost like magic. A trick well worth learning, no matter what math program you use.

Basic Bar Models

All bar model diagrams descend from one basic principle: the whole is the sum of its parts. If you know the value of both parts, you can add them to get the whole. If you know the whole total and one part, you can subtract what you know to find the other part.

Whole	
Part A	Part B

The most basic bar diagram: Two parts make a whole.

Suppose we had a problem like this: "How much must I add to 2 to get 7 as the sum?" Would it trick you into saying 2 + 7 = 9?

We can draw a rectangular bar to represent the total amount. Then we divide it into two parts, representing the number we know and the unknown part. Now it's easy to see the answer:

7

2	?

Seven is the sum, the whole thing.
What must be the missing part?

Drawing Tougher Puzzles

As the number relationships in math problems become more complex, the bar may be split into more than two parts. Also, the parts may relate to each other in ways that require a more elaborate diagram. Multiplication, division, or fraction problems will involve several parts that are the same size, called *units*. But even with a complicated story, the solution begins by drawing a simple bar to represent one whole thing.

For instance: "There are 21 girls in a class. There are 3 times as many girls as boys. How many boys are in the class?"

To show three times as many girls as boys, we can start with a bar for the number of boys. That will be one unit, and then we need three units to show the number of girls.

Boys | ? |

Girls | | | |

21

The bar model helps us see that we need to divide,
not multiply, to find the number of boys.

Master These Two Rules

When you want to draw a bar diagram, start with long rectangles—imagine Lego blocks or Cuisenaire rods. Think of the bar as all of the books/fish/snowballs from your story set out in a row.

We write labels beside each bar, to identify its meaning in the story. We may write numbers inside a block and use brackets to group the bars together or to indicate a specific section of a bar.

If you have trouble figuring out where the numbers go in the diagram, ask yourself, "Which is the big amount, the whole thing? What are the parts?"

You must learn two simple but important rules:

The Whole Is the Sum of Its Parts

Bar diagrams rely on the inverse relationship between addition and subtraction: The whole is the sum of its parts. No matter how complicated the word problem, the solution begins by identifying a whole thing made up of parts.

Simplify to a Single Unknown

You cannot solve for two unknown numbers at once. You must use the facts given in your problem and manipulate the blocks in your drawing until you can connect one unknown unit (or a group of same-size units) to a number. Once you find that single unknown unit, the other quantities will fall into place.

Practice until drawing a diagram becomes almost automatic. Start with simple story problems that are easy enough to solve with a flash of insight. Figure out how you can show the relationships between quantities, translating the English of the stories into a bar model picture. Then work up to more challenging problems.

The following chapters provide a range of story puzzles from early-elementary problems to middle-school stumpers. For answers and fully worked-out solutions, see the companion book *Word Problems from Literature: An Introduction to Bar Model Diagrams.*

Lay the Foundation: One-Step Problems with Mr. Popper's Penguins

The Voice in the Air

During the winter, Mr. Popper read 34 books about Antarctica. Then he read 5 books about penguins. How many books did Mr. Popper read in all?

Greta

When Mr. Popper opened the windows and let snow come into the living room, his children made snowballs. Janie made 18 snowballs. Bill made 14 more than Janie did. How many snowballs did Bill make? How many snowballs did the children make altogether?

More Mouths to Feed

Mr. Popper had 78 fish. The penguins ate 40 of them. How many fish did Mr. Popper have left?

Mr. Greenbaum

The family dressed in their best clothes for their meeting with Mr. Greenbaum. Mrs. Popper had a ribbon 90 centimeters long. She had 35 cm left after making a bow for Janie. How much ribbon did Mrs. Popper use to make the bow?

On the Road

Popper's Performing Penguins did theater shows for 2 weeks. They performed 4 shows every week. How many shows did the penguins perform?

Fame

While they were staying at the hotel, Mr. Popper put a leash on Captain Cook and took him for a walk. They climbed up 3 flights of stairs. There were 10 steps in each flight. Then Captain Cook flopped onto his stomach and slid down all the stairs. He pulled Mr. Popper with him all the way. How many steps did Mr. Popper fall down?

Build Modeling Skills: Multistep Problems with Ben Franklin

Milk Street—Boston, 1706

Ben helped his father make 650 tallow candles. After selling some, they had 39 candles left. How many candles did they sell?

Printer's Ink—1718

Ben sold 830 newspapers. His brother James sold 177 fewer newspapers than Ben.

    (a) How many newspapers did James sell?

    (b) How many newspapers did they sell altogether?

The Water American—London, 1724

Ben loved to visit the London book shops. In one small shop, there were 6 shelves of books. Each shelf held the same number of books. There were 30 books altogether. How many books were on each shelf?

A Shop of Your Own—Philadelphia, 1726

Ben and his friends made a club called "The Junto" to read books and discuss ideas. Ben read 7 science books. He read 5 times as many history books as science books. How many more history books than science books did he read?

Industry and Frugality—1732

Ben collected donations of 2,467 pounds in a bank account to start a new hospital. A friend gave him another 133 pounds. How much more money must Ben collect if he needs 3,000 pounds for the hospital?

An American in Paris—1776–1785

While in France to negotiate a treaty, Ben went to a fancy party. There were 1,930 women at the party. There were 859 fewer men than women. How many people were at the party altogether?

Master the Technique:
From Multiplication
to Fractions
in Narnia

Tea with Mr. Tumnus

Mr. Tumnus told Lucy about a midnight party of fauns and dryads in the forest of Narnia. 35 fauns came to the party. There were 3 times as many dryads as fauns. How many creatures were at the party? If the whole group split equally into 5 large circles for dancing, how many were in each circle?

Back on This Side of the Door

The Professor had 486 books at his house, some in the library room and some in his study. There were 50 books more in the library than in the Professor's study. How many books were in the study?

In the Witch's House

The White Witch had 300 servants at her house, which was really a small castle. There were 10 more wolves than red dwarfs. The number of red dwarfs was twice the number of black dwarfs. How many black dwarfs worked at the Witch's house?

A Day with the Beavers

Mrs. Beaver baked a "great and gloriously sticky marmalade roll" for dessert. She cut ⅙ of the roll for her and Mr. Beaver to share, and then she sliced up ⅘ of the roll for the children. What fraction of the marmalade roll was left?

What Happened After Dinner

Mrs. Beaver had a pitcher of milk. She poured ½ of it into glasses for the children to drink with dinner. Then she poured ⅛ of the pitcher into their cups of after-dinner tea. How much of the pitcher of milk did Mrs. Beaver use?

The Spell Begins to Break

The Witch's sledge got stuck in the mud and slush 24 times before she gave up and decided to walk. ⅔ of those times, the Witch made Edmund get out and help push. How many times did Edmund have to push the sledge?

Peter's First Battle I

⅖ of the creatures waiting with Aslan at his pavilion beside the Stone Table were dryads and naiads. There were 20 dryads and naiads in all. How many creatures were waiting with Aslan at his pavilion?

Peter's First Battle II

Aslan sent 20 of the swiftest creatures to follow the wolf and rescue Edmund. ⅖ of these creatures were eagles, griffins, and other flying fighters. The rest were centaurs, leopards, and other fast-running beasts. How many of the creatures that Aslan sent could not fly?

The Triumph of the Witch

The White Witch's evil minions used 4 ⅖ meters of rope to bind Aslan's legs together. They used ³⁄₁₀ m less of rope to tie him tightly to the Stone Table. How many meters of rope did the wicked creatures use in all?

At Cair Paravel by the Sea

⅘ of the sea people who sang and played music for the coronation party were mermen. If there were 8 mermaids, how many sea people performed at the party?

Reap the Reward:
Ratios and More Fractions
in Middle Earth

An Unexpected Party

Bilbo had 3 times as many apple tarts as mince pies in his larder. If he had 24 more apple tarts than mince pies, how many of the pastries (both tarts and pies) did he have altogether?

Roast Mutton

The three trolls had 123 pieces of gold. Tom had 15 pieces of gold more than Bert. Bert had 3 pieces fewer than William. How many pieces of gold did William have?

Over Hill and Under Hill

The Great Goblin had twice as many goblin soldiers as his cousin, the Gross Goblin. How many soldiers must the Great Goblin send to his cousin so that they will each have 1,200 goblin soldiers?

Riddles in the Dark

Gollum caught 10 small fish. He divided the fish to make 4 equal meals.
How many fish did he eat at each meal?

Queer Lodgings

Beorn baked a large loaf of whole-grain bread. He ate ⅓ of the loaf himself (with plenty of honey!), and he sliced ½ of the same loaf to feed the dwarfs and Bilbo. What fraction of the loaf was left?

Barrels Out of Bond

The Elvenking had a barrel of fine wine. His butler poured ¾ gallon of it into a small keg. He drank ½ of the keg and gave the other half to his friend, the chief of the guards. How much wine did the Elvenking's butler drink?

Inside Information

⅔ of the items in the dragon Smaug's treasure were made of gold. ¼ of the remaining part was precious gems. What fraction of Smaug's treasure was precious gems?

The Battle of Five Armies, Part 1

When the Elvenking heard the dragon had been killed, he set out to claim a share of the treasure. ⅖ of his army were archers. ½ of the remainder fought with spears, and the rest carried swords. If 300 soldiers carried swords, how many elves marched out with the Elvenking?

The Battle of Five Armies, Part 2

The bowman Bard gathered a small army of 600 survivors from the town of Esgaroth, which the dragon had destroyed. The ratio of archers to swordsmen was 2:3. How many archers followed Bard to the Lonely Mountain?

The Return Journey

The dwarfs rewarded Bilbo with two chests of gold, silver, and small gems—6,000 pieces of treasure altogether. There were twice as many pieces of gold as there were gems. There were 600 more pieces of silver than gems. How much of each type of treasure did Bilbo receive?

A Long-Expected Party

Gandalf loaded so many fireworks into his cart for Bilbo's birthday party that he only had time to shoot off ⅗ of them. If he blasted 72 fireworks during the party, how many did he bring in his cart?

A Conspiracy Unmasked

Frodo and his four friends (Sam, Merry, Pippin, and the oft-forgotten Fatty Bolger) enjoyed one last meal before setting off on the Quest of the Ring. If the hobbits shared equally all 135 sausages in the larder, how many sausages did each hobbit eat?

Fog on the Barrow-Downs

The hobbits shared two loaves of bread for their lunch at the Barrow-downs. Frodo wasn't very hungry, so he took a small piece and then split the rest evenly among his friends. If Sam, Pippin, and Merry each received ⅗ of a loaf, what size piece did Frodo eat?

Moving Toward Algebra:
Challenge Problems

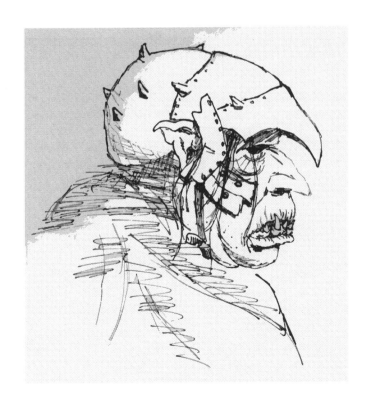

At Helm's Deep

The king of Rohan placed 1,500 guards atop the outer wall at Helm's Deep. 300 of the guards were swordsmen and the rest were archers. How many percent fewer swordsmen were there than archers?

The Well-Dressed Nazgûl

The Dark Lord's tailor has 32 yards of black cloth to make traveling capes for the Ringwraiths. The tailor needs 3 ¾ yards for each cape. How many capes can he make? How much additional cloth will he need to make all 9 capes?

Sauron's Minions

The day before the great battle at the Black Gate, a company of 450 orcs camped among the host of Mordor. But an argument broke out over dinner, and ⅓ of them were killed. Then ⅖ of the remainder died when a drunken troll stumbled through their camp during the night. How many of the orcs survived to join the morning's battle?

In a Galaxy Far, Far Away

Han Solo was doing maintenance work on the Millennium Falcon. He spent ⅗ of his money upgrading the hyperspace motivator. He spent ¾ of the remainder to install a new blaster cannon. If he spent 450 credits altogether, how much money did he have left?

In the Enchanted Forest

Princess Cimorene spent an afternoon cleaning and organizing the dragon's treasure. ¼ of the items she sorted were jewelry. 60% of the remainder were potions, and the rest were magic swords. If there were 48 magic swords, how many pieces of treasure did she sort in all?

Create Your Own
Word Problems

The Story Problem Challenge

WHAT DO YOU GET WHEN you cross a library book with a math worksheet? A great alternative to math homework!

The rules are easy:

(1) Choose your favorite book or movie universe. Think about how the characters might use numbers. What sort of things would they count? Do they use money? Do they build things, or cook meals, or make crafts? Do they need to keep track of how far they have traveled? Or how long it takes to get there?

(2) Choose a worksheet calculation to be the basis for your word problem. Solve the calculation.

(3) Think, "Where in my story would these numbers make sense?"

(4) Write your word problem.

To make the game easier, you may change the numbers to make a more realistic problem, but you must keep the same type of calculation. For instance, if your worksheet problem was $18 \div 3$, you could change it to $18 \div 6$ or $24 \div 3$ to fit your story, but you can't make it something like $18 - 3$.

Things to Consider

Some quantities are discrete and countable, such as hobbits and fireworks. Other quantities are continuous, such as a barrel of wine or a length of fabric. Be sure to consider both types when you are deciding what to use in your problem.

People often think of addition and subtraction as putting together or taking away sets of discrete items. But you can also write stories about growth or comparison—for instance, you might ask how much more or less of something. Or you can use classification, sorting the people or items in your story into groups, and one group might be bigger or smaller than the other.

People often think of multiplication and division as counting or splitting groups of items. But you can also think of things that grow or shrink, so their new size is some number of times as big or small as before. And don't forget rates and ratios—like sausages per hobbit or yards of cloth per cape.

If you are working with fractions, think about sharing something continuous, like pizza or fabric, or shrinking something to a fraction of its original size. For decimals, you'll probably want stories about measurements or about money.

...and may the Math be with you!

About the Author

DENISE GASKINS ENJOYS MATH, AND she delights in sharing that joy with young people. "Math is not just rules and rote memory," she says. "Math is like ice cream, with more flavors than you can imagine. And if all you ever do is textbook math, that's like eating broccoli-flavored ice cream."

A veteran homeschooling mother of five, Denise has taught or tutored mathematics at every level from pre-K to undergraduate physics "which," she explains, "at least in the recitation class I taught, was just one story problem after another. What fun!"

Now she writes the popular blog Let's Play Math at DeniseGaskins.com and manages the Math Teachers at Play monthly math education blog carnival.

A Note from Denise

I hope you enjoyed this Playful Math Singles *book and found new ideas that make learning fun.*

If you believe this book is worth sharing, please consider posting a review at Goodreads.com or at your favorite bookseller's website. Just a few lines would be great. An honest review is the highest compliment you can pay to any author, and your comments help fellow readers discover good books.

Thank you!

—DENISE GASKINS
LETSPLAYMATH@GMAIL.COM

Fantasy Novels by Teresa Gaskins

The Riddled Stone Series
tabletopacademy.net/fantasy-fiction

Banished: Who Stole the Magic Shard?

All Christopher Fredrico wanted was to be a peaceful scholar who could spend a lot of time with his friends. Now, falsely accused of stealing a magical artifact, Chris is forced to leave the only home he knows.

But as he and his friends travel towards the coast, they find a riddle that may save a kingdom—or cost them their lives.

Hunted: Magic is a Dangerous Guide

As a child, Terrin of Xell was almost devoured by a spirit from the Dark Forest. She knows better than to trust magic. But when her friend Chris was accused of a magical crime he didn't commit, she couldn't let him face banishment alone.

So she and her friends get caught up in a quest to recover an ancient relic, with only magic to guide them. And everything is going wrong.

Betrayed: How Can a Knight Fight Magic?

Trained by the greatest knight in North Raec, Sir Arnold Fredrico dreamed of valiant deeds. Save the damsel. Serve the king.

Dreams change. Now the land teeters at the brink of war. As a fugitive with a price on his head, Arnold struggles to protect his friends.

But his enemy wields more power than the young knight can imagine.

45134123R00050

Made in the USA
Columbia, SC
20 December 2018